This Book Belongs to

_____

Table of Contents

My Personal Information

Legal Name ....

Maiden Name / Other Names ....

Social Security Number ....

Birthplace ....

Address ....

....

....

P.O. Box number ....

P.O. Box key is located ....

....

Phone Numbers ....

....

National Insurance Number ....

National Health Number ....

Tax Reference Number ....

Passport Number ....

Driving License Number ....

Other Details

....

....

....

....

....

....

....

....

....

....

....

....

....

....

....

....

List of Important Contacts & People to be Notified

Name ....

Relationship ....

Phone Number ....

Email ....

Name ....

Relationship ....

Phone Number ....

Email ....

Name ....

Relationship ....

Phone Number ....

Email ....

Name ....

Relationship ....

Phone Number ....

Email ....

Name ....

Relationship ....

Phone Number ....

Email ....

Name ....

Relationship ....

Phone Number ....

Email ....

Name ....

Relationship ....

Phone Number ....

Email ....

Name ....

Relationship ....

Phone Number ....

Email ....

Name ....

Relationship ....

Phone Number ....

Email ....

Name ....

Relationship ....

Phone Number ....

Email ....

List of Important Contacts & People to be Notified

Name ....

Relationship ....

Phone Number ....

Email ....

Name ....

Relationship ....

Phone Number ....

Email ....

Name ....

Relationship ....

Phone Number ....

Email ....

Name ....

Relationship ....

Phone Number ....

Email ....

Name ....

Relationship ....

Phone Number ....

Email ....

Name ....

Relationship ....

Phone Number ....

Email ....

Name ....

Relationship ....

Phone Number ....

Email ....

Name ....

Relationship ....

Phone Number ....

Email ....

Name ....

Relationship ....

Phone Number ....

Email ....

Name ....

Relationship ....

Phone Number ....

Email ....

Funeral Wishes & Other Arrangements

Who to Contact ....

....

Burial or Cremation ....

Where? ....

....

Grave Marker ....

Desired Epitaph ....

Funeral Service, what type and where? ....

Who would you like to carry out the Service? ....

Funeral Service readings and music? ....

....

Where would you like the post-gathering to be? ....

....

Guest I Like to Attend My Funeral ....

....

....

....

....

....

....

....

....

....

....

....

....

....

....

....

....

....

....

....

....

....

....

Other Notes on My Funeral ....

....

....

....

....

....

....

....

....

....

....

....

....

....

....

....

....

....

....

....

....

....

....

....

Other Details

Important Documents

I have made a will/testament and it is located ....

My most recent will is dated ....

I have written a letter of wishes and it is located ....

My executors are

Name ....

Address ....

Phone...

Email ....

Name ....

Address ....

Phone...

Email ....

Birth Certificate is located ....

Marriage Certificate is located ....

Passport is located ....

I have a power of attorney, and it is dated ....

It is registered with the Office of the Public Guardian ....

My attorneys are

Name ....

Address ....

Phone...

Email ....

Name ....

Address ....

Phone...

Email ....

Other Details

....

....

....

....

....

....

....

....

....

....

Financial information & Bank Accounts

Financial Documents are located ....

Bank Accounts

Bank Society ....

Account Name ....

Bank Society ....

Account Name ....

Saving Accounts

Bank Society ....

Account Name ....

Bank Society ....

Account Name ....

Mortgage

Bank Society ....

Account Name ....

Credit Cards

Issuer ....

Number ....

Issuer ....

Number ....

Loans

Loan Provider ....

Phone ....

Loan Provider ....

Phone ....

Benefits

Name .... Name ....

Rental agreement

Landlord's Name ....

Phone ....

Other Details

....

....

....

....

....

....

....

....

....

....

....

Properties

Documents Related to Properties are located ....

My House is Own/Rented ....

My Cabin is Own/Rented ....

....

....

....

....

....

....

....

....

....

Other Details

Insurances

Documents Related Insurances are located ....

Life Insurance

Insurance Company ....

Phone ....

Policy Number ....

Health Insurance

Insurance Company ....

Phone ....

Policy Number ....

House Insurance

Insurance Company ....

Phone ....

Policy Number ....

Car Insurance

Insurance Company ....

Phone ....

Policy Number ....

Other Insurance ....

Insurance Company ....

Phone ....

Policy Number ....

Other Details

Utility Providers

Electricity Provider ....

Gas Provider ....

Water Company ....

Broadband Provider ....

Phone Company ....

Mobile Phone Company ....

Television Provider ....

....

....

....

....

....

....

....

....

....

....

....

....

....

....

....

....

Accounts & Passwords, Internet Logins & Passwords

....

....

....

....

....

....

....

....

....

....

....

....

....

....

How to Keep Passwords Safe?

☆ Don't write the most important passwords here, such as your credit card PINs or other bank account login information

☆ You can place important passwords to some secure cloud service which you can let a trusted person to access

☆ Use a password manager which you can let a trusted person to access

☆ Write some hints in this book that your loved ones surely know, so that they can easily understand what the password is

Instructions for Dependents, Pets & Belongings

....

....

....

....

....

....

....

....

....

....

....

....

....

....

....

....

....

....

....

....

....

....

....

....

Other Important Information

....

....

....

....

....

....

....

....

....

....

....

....

....

....

....

....

....

....

....

....

....

....

....

My Final Thoughts

Made in the USA
Las Vegas, NV
06 January 2024

84012279R00024